SCHIRMER'S LIBRARY
OF MUSICAL CLASSICS

Vol. 2080

VIOLIN CLASSICS

12 Pieces by 11 Composers
Advanced Level

For Violin and Piano

ISBN 978-1-4234-2852-7

G. SCHIRMER, Inc.

DISTRIBUTED BY

HAL•LEONARD®
CORPORATION
7777 W. BLUEMOUND RD. P.O. BOX 13819 MILWAUKEE, WI 53213

Visit Hal Leonard Online at
www.halleonard.com

CONTENTS

Allegro moderato

first movement from the Concerto No. 1 in G minor, Op. 26

Edited and fingered by
Henry Schradieck.

Max Bruch
(1838–1920)

6

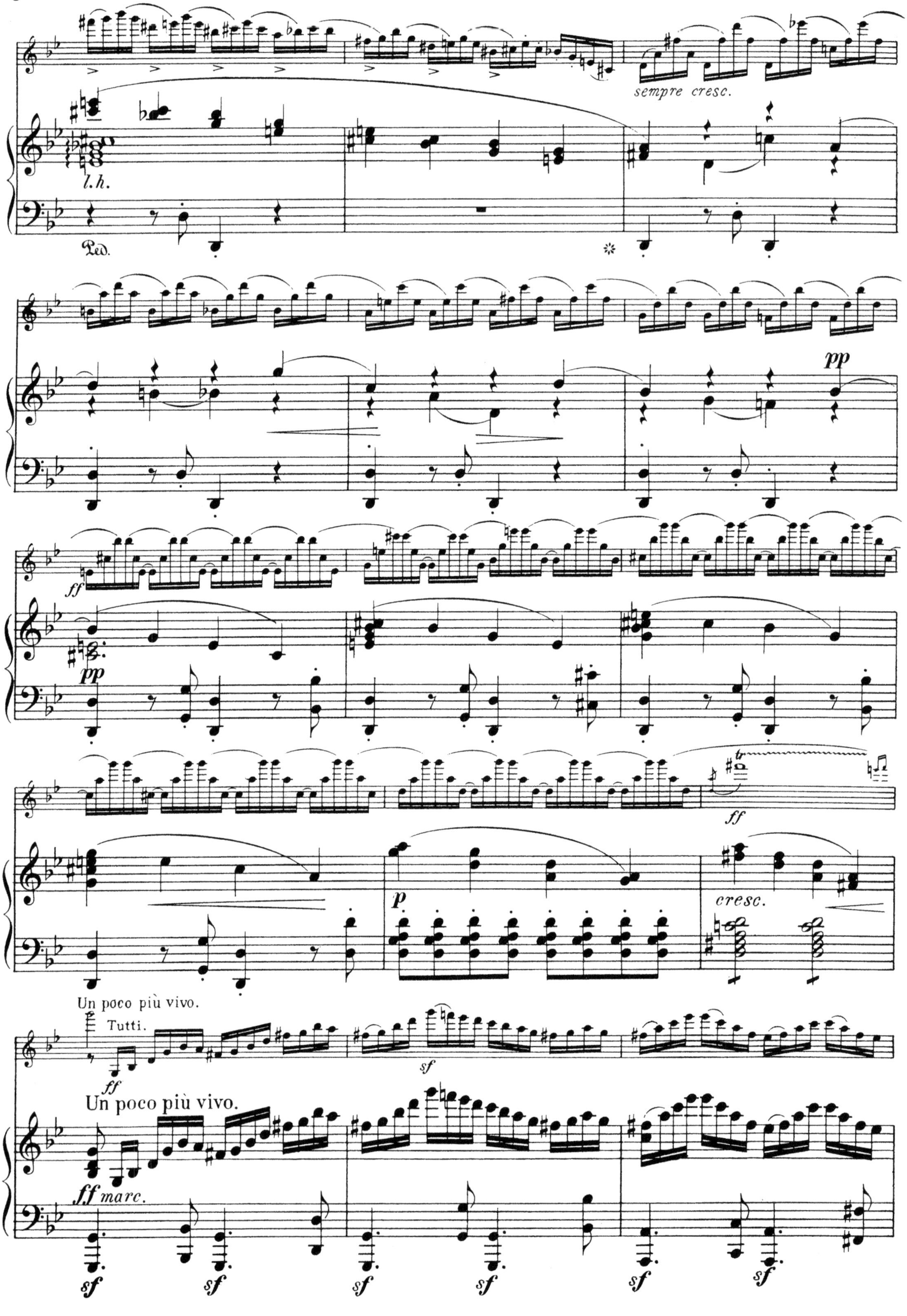
sempre cresc.
l.h.
Ped.
pp
ff
pp
p
cresc.
ff
Un poco più vivo.
Tutti.
ff
sf
Un poco più vivo.
ff marc.
sf

(This page has been intentionally left blank to facilitate page turns.)

Allegro molto appassionato

first movement from the Concerto in E minor, Op. 64

Felix Mendelssohn
(1809–1847)

Cadenza ad libitum.

Romance
Op. 11

Antonín Dvořák
(1841–1904)

Violin part edited by Rok Klopčič

*) ossia:

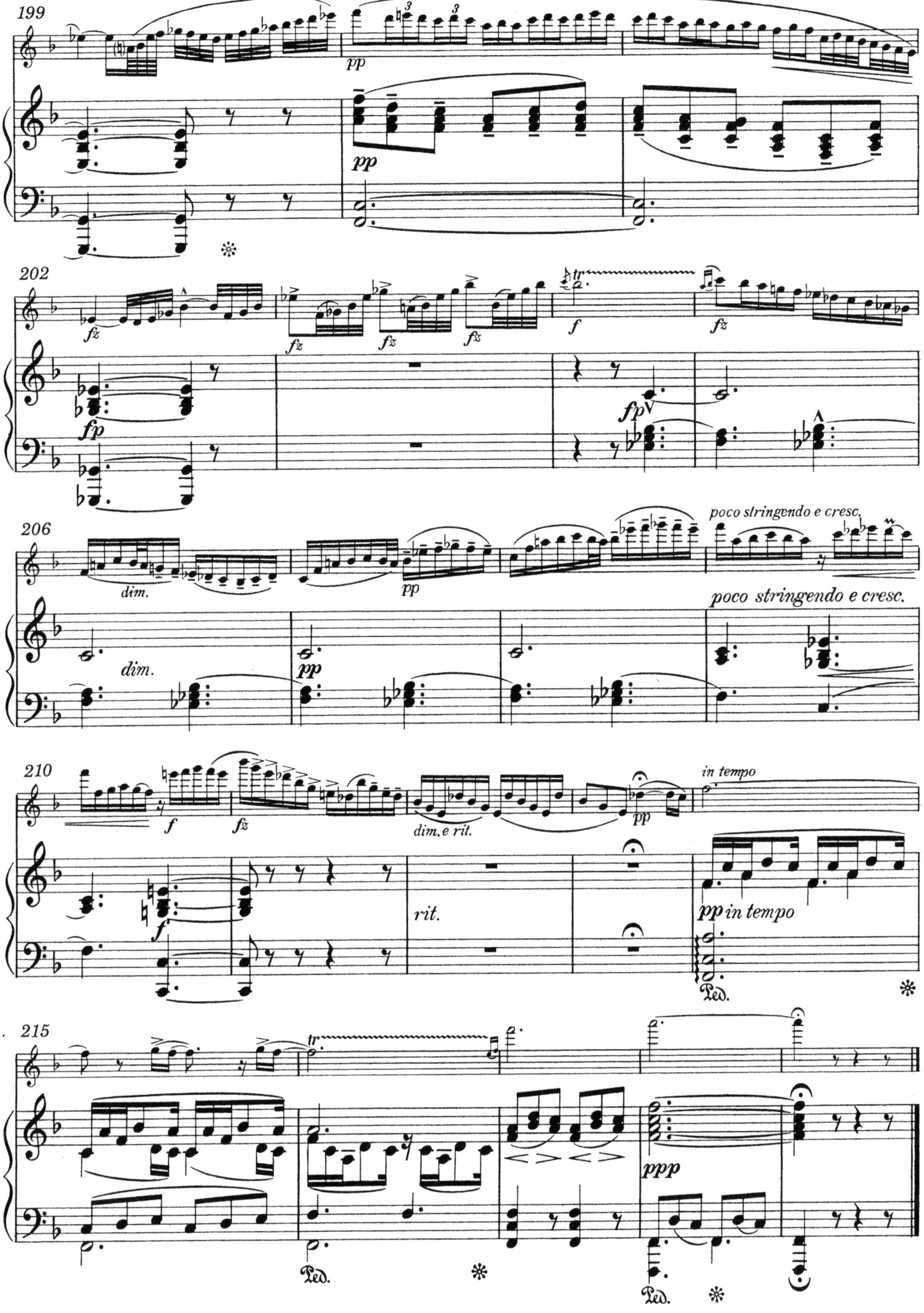
199
pp
202
fz
fp
f
206
dim.
poco stringendo e cresc.
210
dim. e rit.
rit.
in tempo
pp in tempo
215
ppp

Recitativo-Fantasia
third movement from the Sonate in A Major

César Franck
(1822–1890)

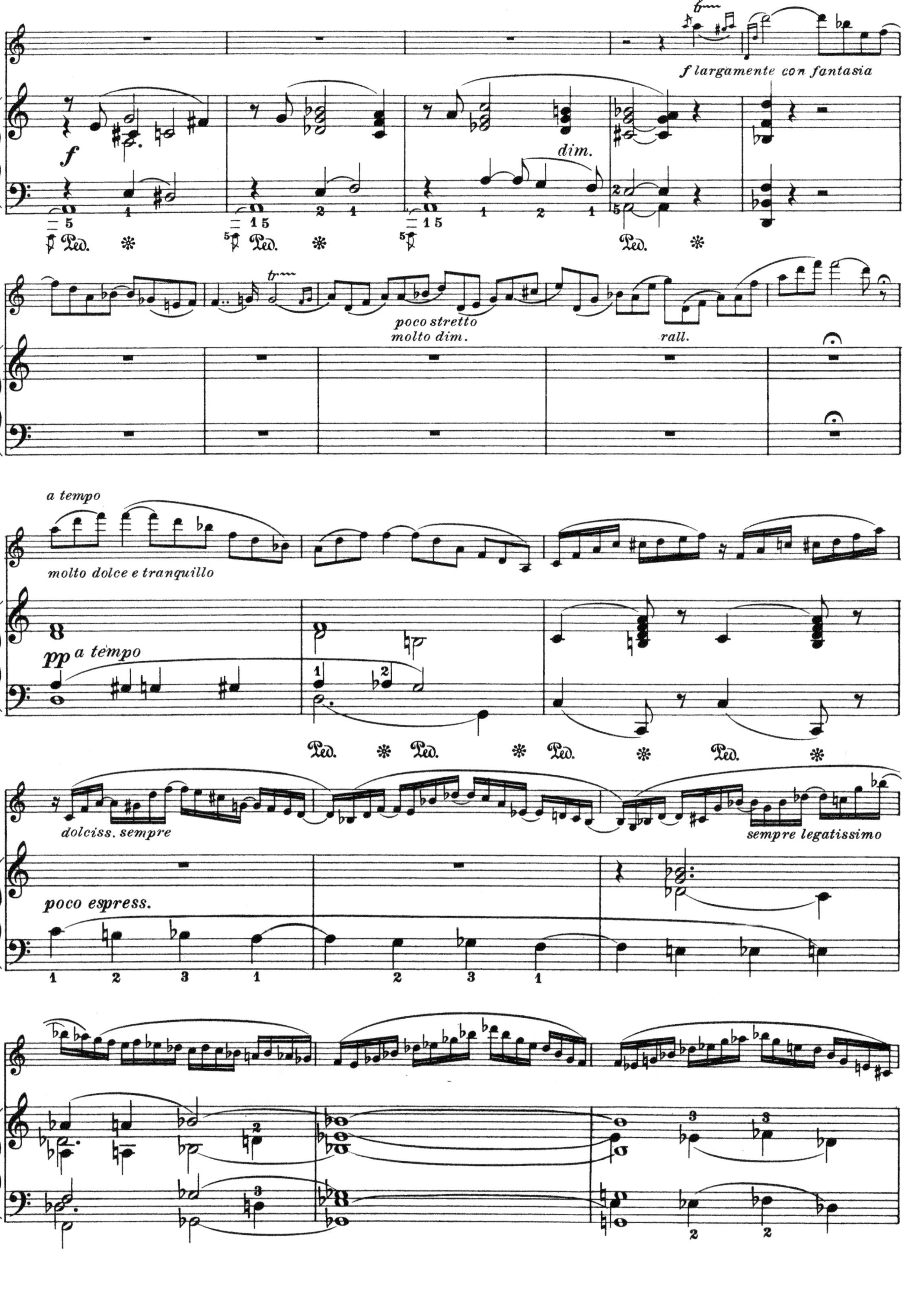
f largamente con fantasia
f
dim.
poco stretto
molto dim.
rall.
a tempo
molto dolce e tranquillo
pp a tempo
dolciss. sempre
sempre legatissimo
poco espress.

Allegro non troppo

first movement from *Symphonie espagnole*, Op. 21

Edited by Leopold Lichtenberg

Édouard Lalo
(1823–1892)

Agitato assai
third movement from the Concerto No. 22 in A minor, G. 97

Giovanni Battista Viotti
(1755–1824)

Scène de Ballet
Op. 100

Charles Auguste de Bériot
(1802–1870)

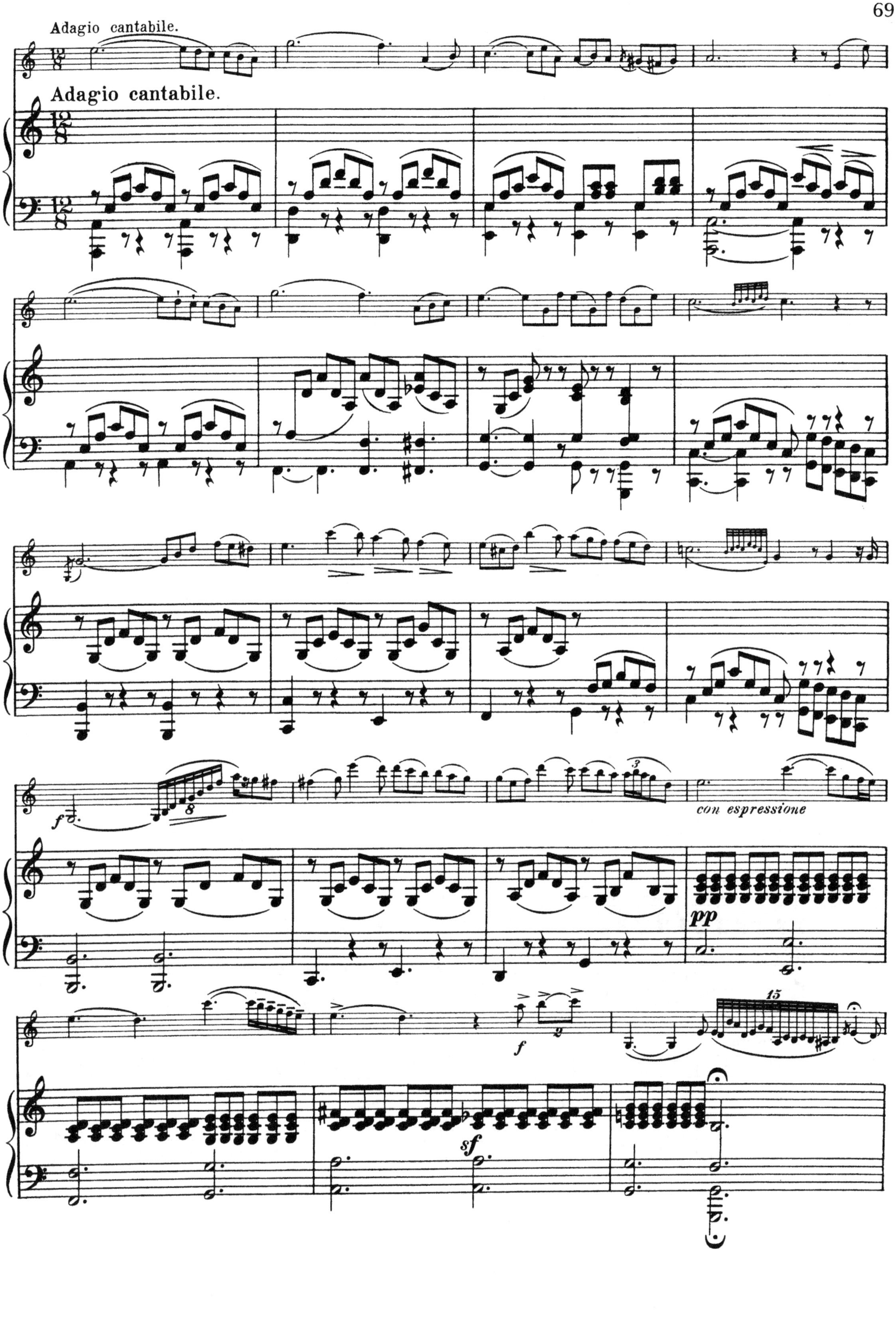
Adagio cantabile.
Adagio cantabile.
f
con espressione
pp
f
sf

Valse moderato.

Valse moderato.

p

poco rall. ——— *dim.*

colla parte

a tempo

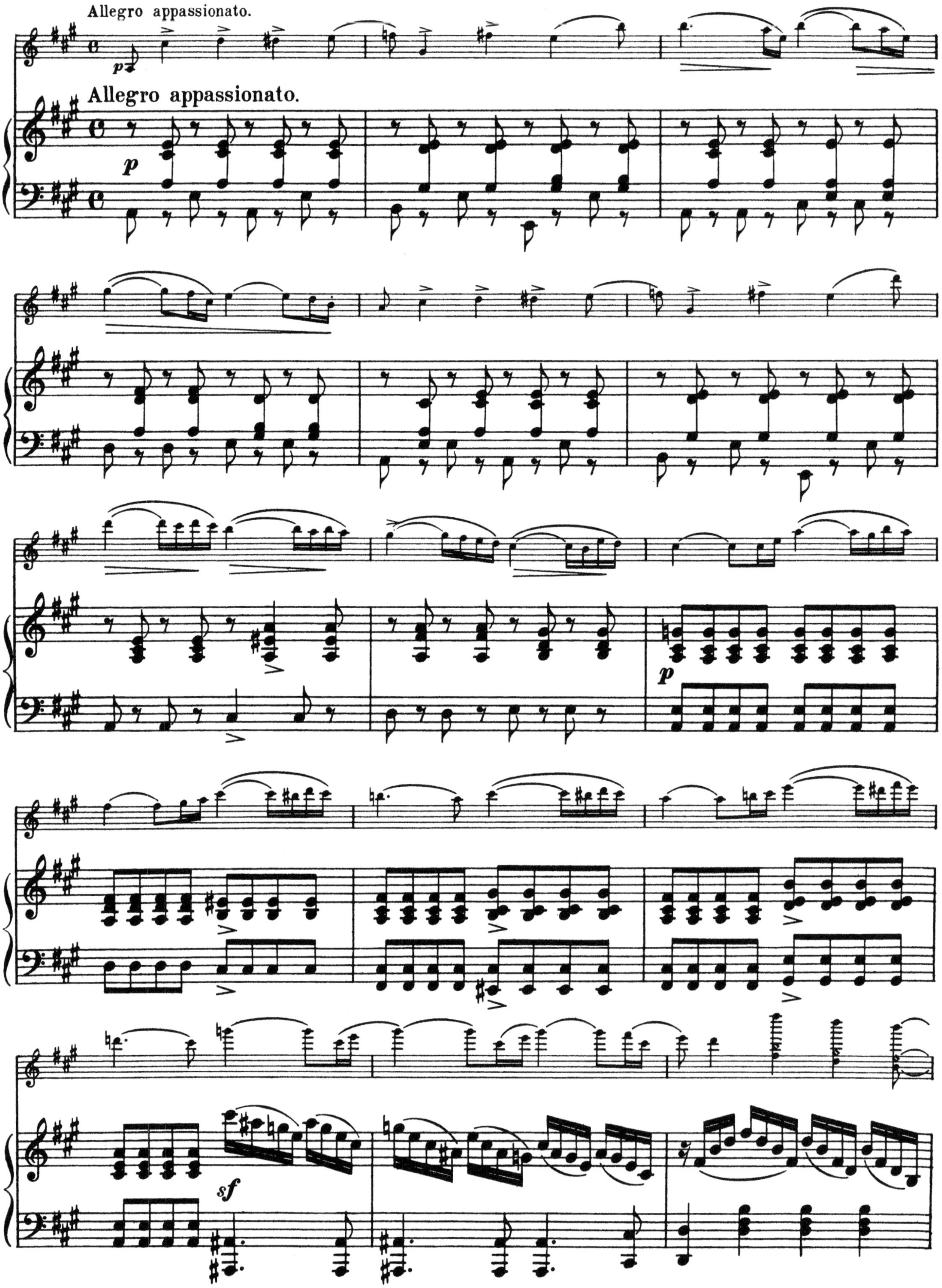
Allegro appassionato.
Allegro appassionato.

(This page has been intentionally left blank to facilitate page turns.)

Rondo
third movement from the Concerto No. 9 in A minor, Op. 104

Charles Auguste de Bériot
(1802–1870)

Concerto in E Major
RV 269 ("Spring")

Piano reduction by Alojz Srebotnjak

Antonio Vivaldi
(1678–1741)

Spring has returned.

SONG OF THE BIRDS

All is gay, and the birds sing happily.

FLOWING FOUNTAINS
Fountains play in the breeze, constantly moving.

THUNDER
The skies are dark; lightning flashes and thunder roars.

SONG OF THE BIRDS

After the storm, the birds return with their song.

On the flowered meadow, the goatherd and his dog roam among the blossoming trees.

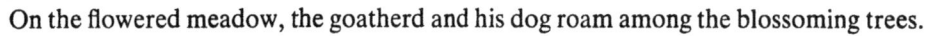

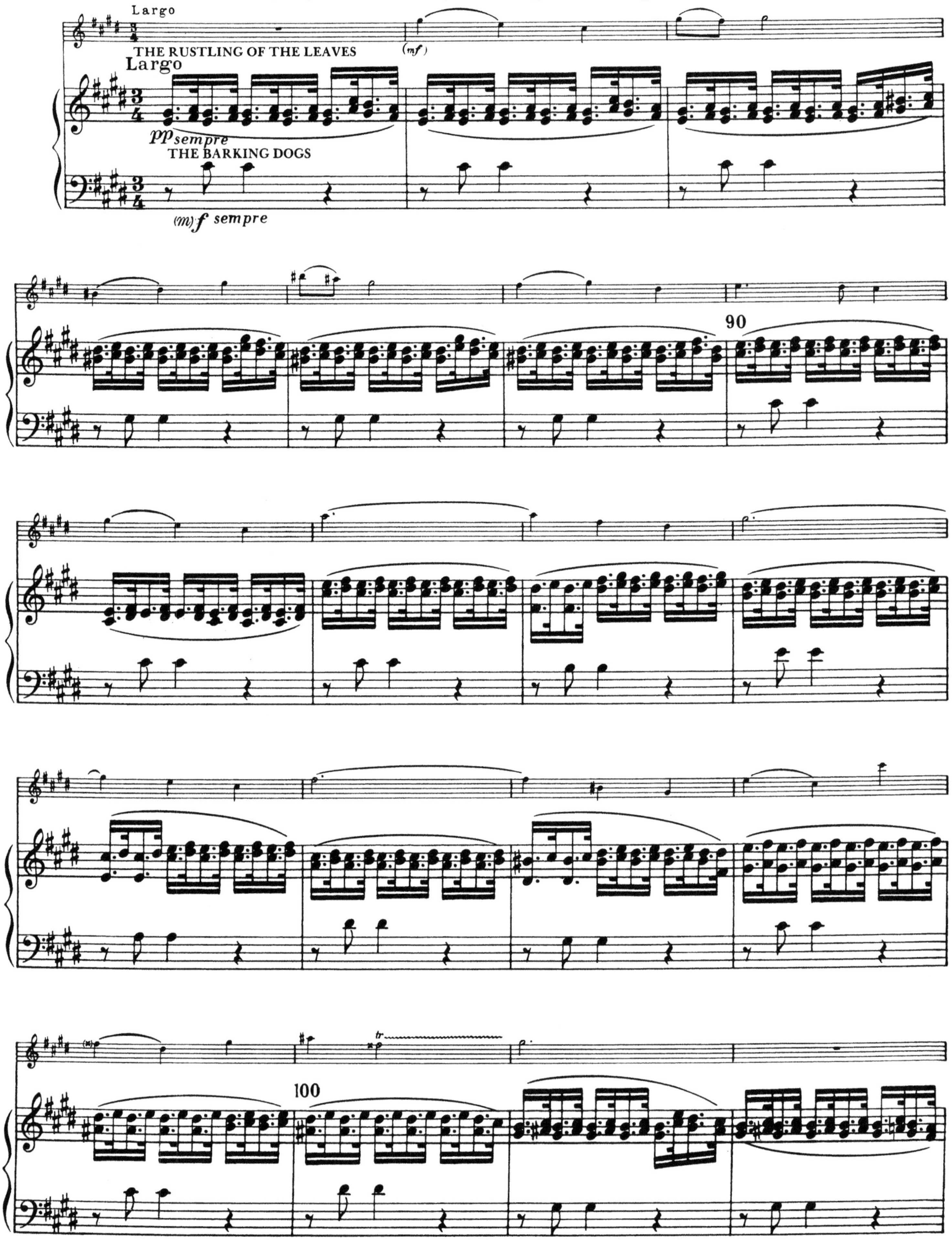

Largo
THE RUSTLING OF THE LEAVES
(mf)
Largo
pp sempre
THE BARKING DOGS
(m)f sempre
90
tr
100

PASTORAL DANCE

Nymphs and shepherds dance to the bagpipes under the beautiful skies of spring.

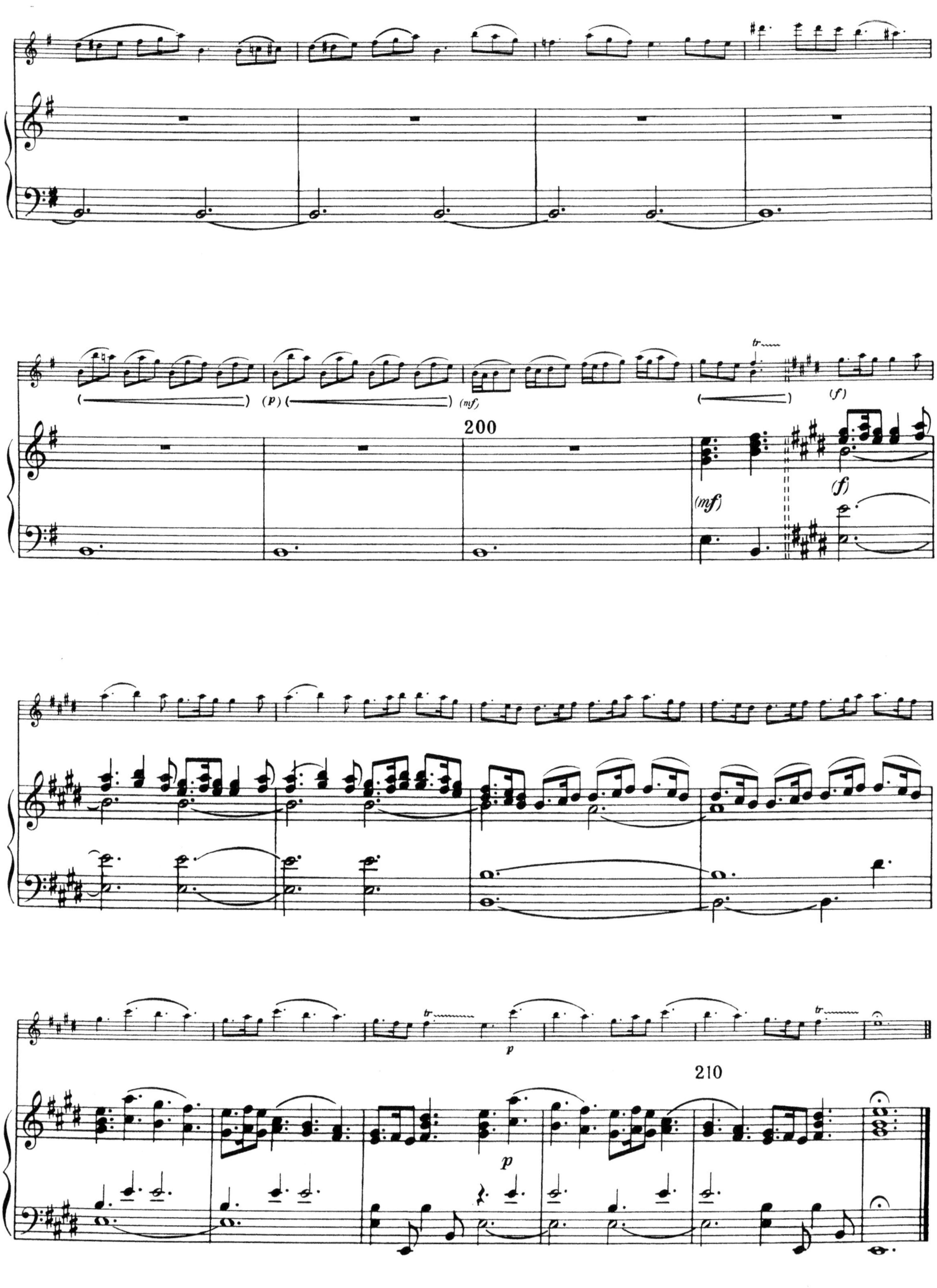
tr
(p)
(mf)
(f)
200
(mf)
(f)
tr
p
210
p
tr

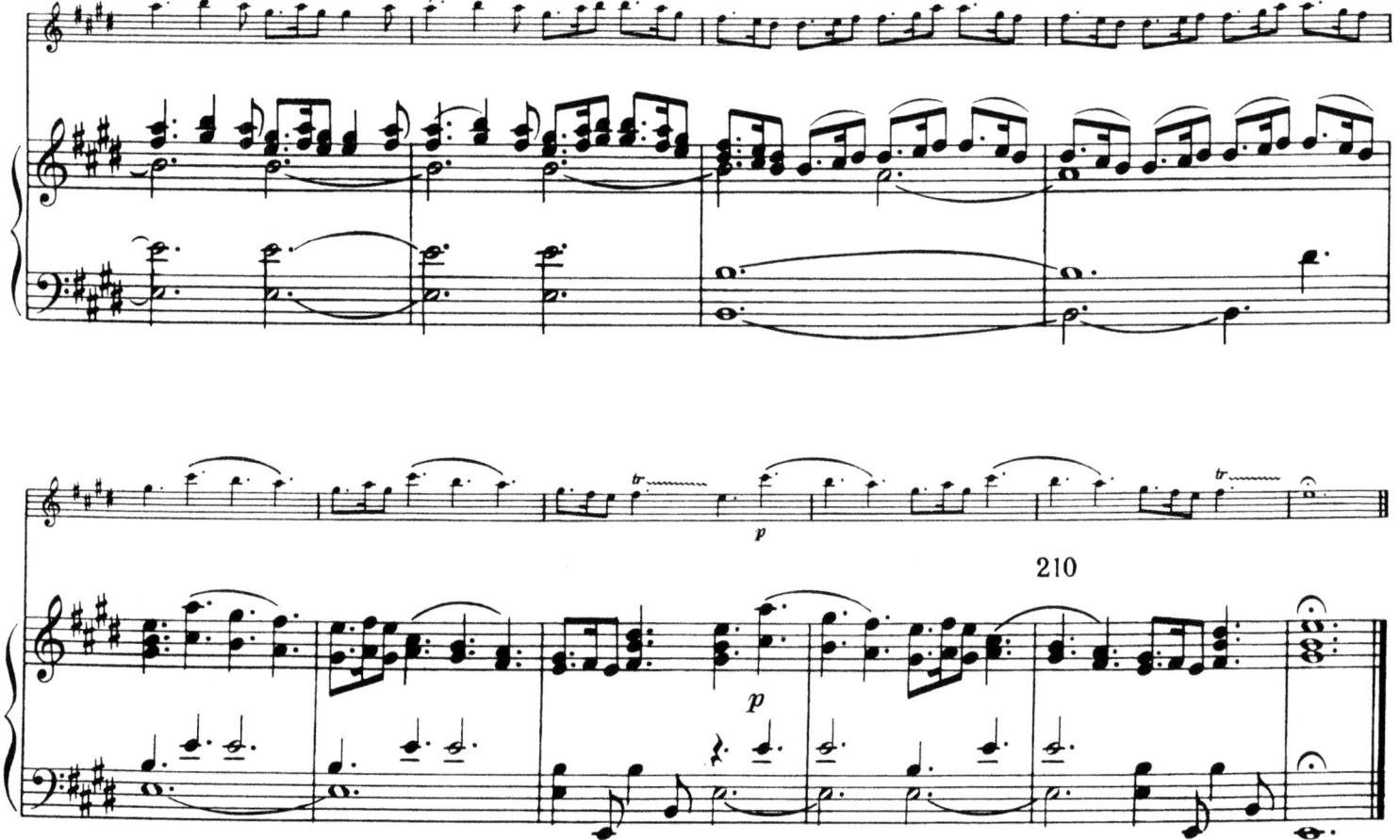

Zigeunerweisen
Op. 20

Edited and fingered by
Philipp Mittell

Pablo de Sarasate
(1844–1908)

Allegro molto vivace